EXODUS

African
POETRY
BOOK SERIES

Series editor: Kwame Dawes

EXODUS

'Gbenga Adeoba

Foreword by Kwame Dawes

University of Nebraska Press / Lincoln

Acknowledgments for the use of copyrighted
material appear on page xix, which constitutes
an extension of the copyright page.

The African Poetry Book Series has been made
possible through the generosity of philanthropists
Laura and Robert F. X. Sillerman, whose
contributions have facilitated the establishment
and operation of the African Poetry Book Fund.

Library of Congress Cataloging-in-Publication Data
Names: Adeoba, 'Gbenga, author. | Dawes,
Kwame Senu Neville, 1962– writer of foreword.
Title: Exodus / 'Gbenga Adeoba;
foreword by Kwame Dawes.
Description: Lincoln: University of Nebraska
Press, [2020] | Series: African poetry book series.
Identifiers: LCCN 2019039021
ISBN 9781496221179 (paperback: alk. paper)
ISBN 9781496221803 (epub)
ISBN 9781496221810 (mobi)
ISBN 9781496221827 (pdf)
Subjects: LCGFT: Poetry.
Classification: LCC PR9387.9.A334 E96 2020
DDC 813/.6—dc23
LC record available at https://lccn.loc.gov/2019039021

Set in Garamond Premier by Mikala R. Kolander.

To Dustin, seafarer, wherever you are!

and

To Peter Akinlabi, with gratitude

CONTENTS

II

FOREWORD

KWAME DAWES

The pull of tides reinvents the shore
into a space for things intimate and lost.
"HERE IS WATER"

In the latter part of this remarkable collection of poems by Nigerian poet 'Gbenga Adeoba, the poet explores memory—personal memory of the meaning of home, of displacement, of exile, and of loss. By then, he has already written one of the most elegant stretches of poetry that explores, with tenderness and power, the function of the imagination in helping us contend with what Toni Morrison argues is the core dilemma of our century, of our time. That if migration and displacement are shaping our ideas of hope, politically and economically, what Adeoba's collection tells us is that today's poet, who is constantly bombarded with images and language about world movements that have a startling impact on the present, must find a language and feeling to write about these things, not out of political necessity, but out of a desperate need for poetry to give a sense of meaning to what is truly present in our world. Adeoba may or may not have read Morrison's essay, but it certainly serves as a remarkably useful context for what he achieves in this collection:

It is a movement of workers, intellectuals, refugees, armies crossing oceans, continents, immigrants through custom offices and hidden routes, speaking multiple languages of trade, of political intervention, of persecution, exile, violence and poverty. There is little doubt that the redistribution (voluntary or involuntary) of people all over the globe tops the agenda of the state, the boardrooms, the neighborhoods, the streets.

Toni Morrison, "The Foreigner's Home" in *The Source of Self-Regard*

With sharply constructed images, with a deep sense of commitment to detail and to an understanding of the spaces he is writing about, Adeoba creates poetry of unmistakable skill and beauty:

On the fortnight of your return,
they would bunch around the evening fire
to learn of your resurrection: the unhallowed season
of the sea, the throes, the convention of birds
on the route where the smugglers
joined you to a truck toward the waters;
and the sovereignty of dust in half-empty towns,
past the caves and their autonomy of green—
foliage retelling parables of no return.
How the sea beyond keeps no record
of the drowned and those it washed ashore,
how you, too, are a Lazarus of the sea.
   ("Resurrection")

One of the great beauties of the poetic craft is the opportunity to be transported and driven and moved by the worlds we encounter. There are many anxieties that should come to us about "globalism" and its implications about imperialism, and about economic and cultural hegemony that not only exploits and commodifies the cultures that are being overwhelmed by the purveyors of globalism, but in some ways it can alienate the people from these cultures of their own cultures. One of the striking things about the emerging African poet is the demonstration of a certain access to the wider world, its influence and culture, its tragedies and trends. The dangers of this kind of access are that the landscape, the culture, and the world outside their doors can be ignored and seen to be not of value. 'Gbenga Adeoba opens his collection with a poem that brilliantly demonstrates how effectively these wider worlds can be engaged, and how the sense of place, of identity are not compromised.

> What binds us,
> in this boat, is a known fear,
> a kinship of likely loss,
>
> the understanding that we, too,
> could become a band of unnamed migrants
> found floating on the face of the sea.
>   ("Seafarers")

Adeoba's capacity for empathy is managed by a resistance to the polemical. He understands the quite necessary art of the poet in search of meaning, which is to enter, as much as possible, into the imagined spaces. Here he engages the Italian coastguard who discovers the body of a Nigerian boy caught in the "shroud of a wave" on the coast. Adeoba then reiterates the point of empathy and urgency, the shared human sense of loss, and the overwhelming weight of history.

> An old photograph,
> sewn into the inner pocket
> of his caftan, offers a reel
> from his past:
> he, barefooted on a football field,
> in the jersey of an Italian team;
>
> the half smile on his face,
> like a butterfly with one wing,
>
> almost beautiful.
>   ("Nightshift at the Coast")

The ironies have a delicate pain, a football fan of an Italian team, a figure caught in the global contradictions of migration and exile, the economic and

cultural quagmire that dominates the world that fascinates Adeoba. Toni
Morrison's sharply focused reflections on globalism come to mind in this work.

> They crowd the back,
> shrouded in a half light
> haloing their bodies—
> the broken windows
> opening into Asmara,
> Raqqa, Darfur, and other
> cathedrals of war.
>   ("Leaving Agadez")

Adeoba sets himself a challenge of writing a poetry of empathy for a grand
phenomenon, a philosophical concept that has grave personal implications for so
many. In this sense, Adeoba's project is deeply political and immediate in its impli-
cations. Yet what he manages to achieve is a tenderness of feeling and a complex of
emotion without losing sight of the politics of the work. He finds ways to connect
the plights of migrants and refugees from around the world, from Haiti to Nigeria
to Libya to Italy and even to centuries before, to 1761 on a ship crossing the Middle
Passage—they are a people who are being defined by the need to move before the
inadequacies of where they are, or who are being forced to move because of the
pull of factories, of dirty streets, of farms, of the needs of the wealthier nations—a
kind of slavery. In "Chorography" he takes us to a coastal village in Nigeria with
its "Passels of fishing boats / and canoes," and he contends with his role as a kind
of "chorographer," a mapper of circumstance and outrage. His role is not merely
to list these tragedies, to be a demographer, but instead to find, through poetry, an
"intimation," if you will, a way to humanize the experience:

> No demographer can intimate
> a census of this country
> upon the waters.
>
> Across the meld, broken women,
> bonded by fish trade, bunch

around a peer who lost her husband
to the evictors' fire.

And yet, what deepens the pain of these accountings is the language of bureaucracy, the almost passive impersonality of that language: "peer," "evictor," "broken women." And yet, he presses against the dulling of the impersonal, the generic—this is the poetry of collective hurt and psychic pain:

Wailing, the women hurl curses
into the dark; their tender hearts,
the flame in their eyes
probing their peer's silence,

the ache beyond,
and the uncertainty of days
still to come.

Adeoba establishes that complex of feeling by moving between a lyric sense of loss and the collective sense of communal loss. In the very next poem, "A Funeral Hymn in Falsetto," he speaks of the death of his grandfather. The language is as controlled and deliberate as everything that Adeoba writes:

At the funeral,
when the chorister sang
the paradise hymn in falsetto,
I imagined a brood of angels
heralding the arrival of my grandfather
who was migrating in a boat of glass.

He turns to the image of boats to speak of his grandfather's journey. In this instance, the boat of departure, the boat of exile, is a glass one, and at least, in this instance, there is a faithful heralding of his grandfather's arrival at home. Of course, it is ironic, and it is troubled. The hope here is "imagined" and this too is extremely important. And this is the dance that undergirds this collection. A poet in search of the language of hope that is collective and tender and beautiful and yet never losing sight of the reality of the experience, the politics of a world showing no mercy toward itself. Adeoba does not attempt to analyze the details of the politics, does not seek to present a discourse on the hows and whys. What he is doing is mapping the effect of these things— it's a prophet's task, the task of a witness, the poet's task that is distinguished by the quest for beauty—the faith in the imagination. In "What Birds Sing of in Libya," he makes two strong appeals:

> The sheer miracle of aves
> urging men to love again, calling
> them to images craving tenderness:
> . . . .
> preach love yet again,
> and call humanity
> to the loss of itself.

Later, Adeoba continues the discourse established so eloquently by Toni Morrison in evoking one of the great and defining migrations of the last millennium, the Atlantic slave trade. Even then, the imagination must find its saving power—and songs, for Adeoba, whether birdsongs, funeral songs, or hymns, are the transformative forces of hope.

> No daily had enough room for this loss, those slaves
> huddled in the ship cell as a cluster, singing,
> knitting their singsong into the thick of that hurricane.
> ("Middle Passage")

Adeoba's indebtedness to Derek Walcott is most apparent in his genuine fascination with the sea or bodies of water. The collection may well have been called "The Sea Is History," but for Adeoba, as for Walcott, it is more than history—it is the source of language and metaphor that holds the work together, and in the various ways Adeoba invokes the water, he enacts something of a tour de force in focused and beautifully conceived language. At his best, Adeoba threads images of the sea into his exploration of the people these poems are about. In "Eclipse," a poem that takes him to what he describes as a slave port in Dahomey, he speaks of the urgency of the sea, an urgency that speaks to the hope of freedom and the terrible trap of enslavement—at once loose and narrow:

> There seemed to be an urgency on the sea,
> a rhythm of narrowness,
> and it was unlike the tune they had learnt:
> to be wide and free like this water.
> Ripples, too, the sheer liturgy of liquid bodies.
> Held within the crevices of each ripple
> were tossed dreams, rehearsed scenes
> and unheard songs, the lexicon of memory
> and wisdom told in Bariba, Fon, and Fula,
> unwinding, reeling into that Dahomeyan pallor
> and the soft pockets of the sea.

And in this, and in poems like "Pa Cudjo Lewis Weaves a Song," "Desert Fathers," and "A Short Essay on Drowning," we understand at once that Adeoba is—by dint of learning, of access to information, and above all, by dint of the imagination—a poet of Africa and the diaspora. In his hands, this is not a political or ideological moniker but a triumph of the imagination, and the imagination allows him to move through time and space: that voyage across the Atlantic, / from Accra to Black River, / Jamaica, circa 1781" ("A Short Essay on Drowning").

In the end, Adeoba writes with studied care a lyric of absence. In many ways it seems to be a throwback to arch-modernism, to what T. S. Eliot would admire. We see this control and discipline in the ways in which Adeoba relies on the second person in poems like "War Note" and "Nightfall, Aleppo"—at once an address to some unnamed figure and at the same time hinting at a guarded reference to the self. If there is feeling, it is well managed.

You remember that evening,
yet again, the dark witness:

how they dragged your mother
into the night, like they
took your rebel father;

her voice, keen, rising
and failing like something
tethered to the wind.
  ("Nightfall, Aleppo")

It is possible that we won't find in Adeoba's biography a narrative of a
mother dragged into the night and a "rebel father," and importantly, it does not
appear to matter much to Adeoba and to the project he completes here. The
poet's permission lies in imagination, and beyond that, it lies in his capacity to
present the stories of exile and loss in convincing language. Yet, as if to at once
present to us a sense of his aesthetic and to offer us a quality of vulnerability
that he manages with care throughout, Adeoba ends the collection with a
poem of metaphorical intensity and meaning. The artist must negotiate his
or her role in the backward glance. We need not ask where the poet is in this
scenario—he makes things quite clear.

I take an evening walk toward this park
with plains like the memories of Sodom.

I do not lose my identity:
I am neither Lot nor the women;

so, I can afford to look back several times.
There are no pillars of salt,

only juvenile lovers radioing
their passions on short wavelength.
  ("Promenade")

'Gbenga Adeoba's *Exodus* joins a growing body of powerful and necessary engagements with the ideas of exile and migration that Morrison argues, convincingly, is the defining reality of our time. Three that come to mind are Aracelis Girmay's *Black Maria*, Josué Guébo's *Think of Lampedusa*, and Tanella Boni's *The Future Has an Appointment with the Dawn*. Adeoba's book gives us new dimensions to this phenomenon. And in his own way, he is working through his own movement, his own sense of displacement, and his own embrace of the imagination, as a way to find meaning in this.

ACKNOWLEDGMENTS

Acknowledgment is due to the editors of the following publications where many of these poems appeared in different forms or with different titles: *African American Review, Connotations Press, Harpur Palate, Hotel Amerika, Notre Dame Review, Oxford Poetry, Pleiades, Poet Lore, Prairie Schooner*, and *Salamander*. Some of the poems also appeared in the chapbook "Here is Water" included in *New-Generation African Poets: A Chapbook Box Set (Sita)*, edited by Kwame Dawes and Chris Abani.

EXODUS

The sea is History

DEREK WALCOTT

Resurrection

along the coast of Northern Africa

On the fortnight of your return,
they would bunch around the evening fire
to learn of your resurrection: the unhallowed season
of the sea, the throes, the convention of birds
on the route where the smugglers
joined you to a truck toward the waters;
and the sovereignty of dust in half-empty towns,
past the caves and their autonomy of green—
foliage retelling parables of no return.
How the sea beyond keeps no record
of the drowned and those it washed ashore,
how you, too, are a Lazarus of the sea.

Seafarers

The refrain of this water
says something is imminent,
says loss is upon us.

Bordered by kelp—
brown murals supple as wool—
and a cloud of winged witnesses,

our boat is somewhere
in the middle of the Mediterranean,
miles and miles from the coast
near Tobruk in Libya,

where we had camped
until the smugglers and the sea
spoke of its fidelity.

It was a soft, fluid tune:
the tender draw of water—

the sea, keen, humming
a promise of calm,
urging us to draw closer,

to unlearn all we thought we knew
about the posture of water.

There are dismembered boat parts,
whole dinghies, too,
shooting out from somewhere
beneath this expanse,

yielding us to catalogs
of told and untold mishaps;

the sea's unfulfilled promises
to those who had knocked on its door,
those who sought to know its ways:

the Nigerian boy
comforting his sister,
after they lost their mother
miles away from Sabratha,

and those with whom
we had camped at the coast,
the ones who drowned overnight
some hundred miles
south of the island of Lampedusa.
What binds us,
in this boat, is a known fear,
a kinship of likely loss,

the understanding that we, too,
could become a band of unnamed migrants
found floating on the face of the sea.

Nightshift at the Coast

In which a coastguard finds a body washed ashore

When we are gone
our lives will continue without us
—JOHN BURNSIDE

This light, the burst
and softness of its insistence,

bidding you to be still, is holding
the expanse in a meld of brown and red.

From the coast,
you can see the weight
of its sheen pressed on cowries
swept ashore, cuddling in seawater.

It is the same trick artificial lights
play on water, daring an undoing.

There is an intimation of memory
in its stance,

this being your fortyish season
of translating the cryptography
of such early lights.

There are no limits
now to the leaves,
blown seaward, yielding,
unfurling their inner lives.
The sea, too, urging a reintroduction,
becoming what you do not know.

When you check the stretch again,
you find him face-first in the shroud of a wave.

The sea, shifting, heralds
its cargo in quick syllables of an onrush,

this body journeying
from the coast of Sabratha,
where the smugglers' dinghies mostly drown.

An old photograph,
sewn into the inner pocket
of his caftan, offers a reel
from his past:
he, barefooted on a football field,
in the jersey of an Italian team;

the half smile on his face,
like a butterfly with one wing,

almost beautiful.

All the Little Lights Going Out

For Alan Kurdi

Between the losses, I, too,
eyes for the little lights going out,
have come to this fold of love to know you,
beyond being Alan, evacuee, scion of Kurdi,
a lost song shrinking the heart at each retelling.
Before home became the mouth of a shark,
you would go with him to those expanses,
sepia lit, observing the ways of men lost at sea,
and the sway, this doubt that often comes with
naming bodies of water. For him and other
refugees calling us, yet again, to your song,
memory is a cargo floating on seawater.

Child of the World

You want to walk on water so bad
or tell your father you know
what it is to sin,
but you let him pile dreams broken on you instead
—KECHI NOMU

Because his father said water,
not words, was the beginning

of all things, the boy sits often
by the river where he was named.

The aloes, ferns, and bulrushes
are, to him, a wall of kindness.

He would bend his ears
to the ensemble of ripples;

or, when the fishermen were
all gone, he would ford the waters

in search of cities where he
could drown his weight of years.

His father said: son, what you seek
to drown is not a name; it is history.

His father said he was named
for the rust of songs, scars of Libya,

and the gray vaults of the sea.
He said he was named

for drowned men the world over,
his watered flax and tulips

that didn't blossom,
the dream of years withering still.

Thresholds

In which I visited my grandfather's house
for the first time after his death

Eleven years after his passing,
I stand at the threshold
of that balcony where he would sit;
the music of his lore, riffling the air
like the lifting of birds;
his voice, in trickles,
undoing the knots of silence.

Half Acre of Water

A mass funeral was held on Friday in Salerno,
Italy, for 26 young Nigerian women who drowned
while trying to cross the Mediterranean Sea.
—SAHARA REPORTERS, NOVEMBER 17, 2017

Gulls, too, are fleeing
that portion where their
bodies were drowned, those
Nigerian women, 26 of them.

They had begun to drown
those many years ago—in homes
that were no longer homes—

long before they,
keen as early birds,
made for the waters

under the dark witness
of nights; when they said
only the sea could bear
the weight of their grief.

They huddle even in death;
their mouths shaped as though
they wanted to say
what we do not know,

how far they had gone,
that November morning,
in the sure calm of dawn,

before the sea, ageless,
    raised the cost of passage.

But there are no words now,

only the fragments
of lived lives flung about
in that half acre of water;

the birds pitching their grief
from a distance,
mourning the loss—

these women that would rest
in the Italy they never knew.

Exodus

Port au Prince, Haiti, 2010

The boys from the other
street held history in trust
like lands under dispute.

They would dictate what we
could say and what must
remain as thoughts,

daring us to revisit the past,
to look into its mirrors, interfacing
it as a bowl of water in light.

I could have sworn that
I saw the wave, slithering,
a height of ten stories or more,
sweep through the streets
as an electric train
would knife through subways.

But there was only enough time
to carve my name
on the door of a church tower,
where our words
became flesh and blood.

In a flash, the street became a scene
from films depicting the creation story,

everything void and without form.
We became spirits hovering over the
untouched parts, seeking survival.

The face of the sea
was of water betraying water:
everything, in a rush,
gathering into ripples.

Yet we left via waterways.

Faces in the ship
wore mascara of earth
and sang thanksgiving hymns
the sum of particles in a teabag.

The boys from the other street
were also there.
But no one argued
about the height of the first wave.

And there were no arguments
or concessions on whether the memories
should become songs and hieroglyphics
inscribed on a sea chest,

or another legend
told over dregs.

Leaving Agadez

They all cling to remains
of safety in this truck careening
toward Sabha in Libya.
They crowd the back,
shrouded in a half light
haloing their bodies—
the broken windows
opening into Asmara,
Raqqa, Darfur, and other
cathedrals of war.
When they collate their aches,
it is in whispers—
a longing to break this ruse,
the pact between the smugglers
and songbirds governing
this region,
the insistence of gusts sweeping
the desert.
Too frail to bear the angst,
the kids on board are crying.
They are asking their parents
if they will make it,
if they all won't be sold
before they get to Sabha,
or Tripoli, where they can
make for the waters.
But the adults are hesitant.
They know they could be sold,
they could get caught
by the guards who would shout

emshi emshi,[1]
deporting them back to Agadez,
to those camps where comrades
who have failed in this quest reside,
often staying awake
in full moons,
mourning dreams forgone.

Chorography

Otodo Gbame, a waterfront community in Lagos, Nigeria

There is a weight of leaving—
refugees fleeing the evictors, their homes,
and the fire to the unknown.

Passels of fishing boats
and canoes map the lagoon
all the way to Orange Island.

The expanse, unlit, narrowed by grief,
holds more human bodies now.

No demographer can intimate
a census of this country
upon the waters.

Across the meld, broken women,
bonded by fish trade, bunch
around a peer who lost her husband
to the evictors' fire.

Wailing, the women hurl curses
into the dark; their tender hearts,
the flame in their eyes
probing their peer's silence,

the ache beyond,
and the uncertainty of days
still to come.

A Funeral Hymn in Falsetto

The eve of the tenth anniversary of my grandfather's passing

On the night my grandfather rejected tea
and offered his last breath instead,
the earth shifted an inch.
And I listened out for a rustle of leaves
or a flash of thunder
amidst the wailers' phonation.

At the funeral,
when the chorister sang
the paradise hymn in falsetto,
I imagined a brood of angels
heralding the arrival of my grandfather
who was migrating in a boat of glass.

It is a decade now,
and sighs have replaced hymns.
The elegies, too, return to me
the way an empty alley
returns our gift of words in multiples.

What Birds Sing of in Libya

after Ross Kemp

In Brak, Surman, and places
in Libya governed by water,

what breaks the night
is mostly songs—

the lilt, the open pulse
of thrushes warbling their songs,
casting their burdens
upon the waters.

The sheer miracle of aves
urging men to love again, calling
them to images craving tenderness:

Migrants, modern slaves,
huddled on little boats,

crossing the Mediterranean—
a grave wide enough for the numbers—
into the unknown,

through the same routes
desert septs took while importing
human commodities into North Africa
three centuries ago.

On tonight's playlist,
there are moving birdsongs

for those that survive
the desert but end up in dinghies
ferrying them to unnamed countries,
to likely death;

some more for women,
hopeful housemaids,
who have their Italy-bound dreams
diverted to desert brothels,

and young men in captive,
crying, praying their ransom.

The flock, unwavering,
dissecting the waters
with their rhythm,

preach love yet again,
and call humanity
to the loss of itself.

Middle Passage

an unreported shipwreck, circa 1761

"Sirs, I perceive that the voyage will be with injury
and much loss, not only of the cargo and the ship,
but also of our lives"
ACTS 27:10

It was nothing like a trainee sailor's imagination
of the sea or the infirmity of rudders.
But it got darker there in that lackluster region
where the vessel, coasting, tuned out of Zanzibar,
where the sail seemed to have given in
to the wind's insistence on a wreck. It would take a slave
or two to pacify this water psalming a ruin.
Maybe it took more: we would later hear of David,
not Livingstone, who lost his fortune (or his fortune lost him).
Dawson too, darling of kings and warlords;
his accordion, chest, and rum dreams.
No daily had enough room for this loss, those slaves
huddled in the ship cell as a cluster, singing,
knitting their singsong into the thick of that hurricane.

Eclipse

at a slave port in Dahomey, old Benin Republic

All night, they had waited for the captain's blast—
an initiation into a ritual, piercing as a dark prophecy—
so that the ship would sail away from the piers
into a future unfolding in fetters.
There seemed to be an urgency on the sea,
a rhythm of narrowness,
and it was unlike the tune they had learnt:
to be wide and free like this water.
Ripples, too, the sheer liturgy of liquid bodies.
Held within the crevices of each ripple
were tossed dreams, rehearsed scenes
and unheard songs, the lexicon of memory
and wisdom told in Bariba, Fon, and Fula,[1]
unwinding, reeling into that Dahomeyan pallor
and the soft pockets of the sea.
And for once, they knew their dreams, too,
would ebb into a patina speaking only in whispers,
the language of a body speaking to itself.

Pa Cudjo Lewis Weaves a Song

A night so weak
it leans on a cane of light,
a lunar index of grief,

he sits still in Alabama's dark,
adrift of the sea of his life,
the waves of loss—

five sons and a daughter
gone in their prime,
lying still in Old Plateau.

Age has pulled a mask on
the face he could call his, the one
his woman, Abile, didn't know.

A Baptist hymn, elegiac,
pedals through Africatown.

He reimagines Bante,
that far home, now,
the unfurling of songs
and riddles told on ledges,
the tongues of fire;

or women, in a loop of grief,
mourning husbands and lost sons,
mornings after they were captured,
herded through tunnels of green,
through Abomey and Ouidah,

to a two-masted schooner
perched on the waters
like a bird in rest.
The boys singing their ache
to the wind.

The hymn, louder now,
wafts into his invented space,
urging a shift from that posture.

He weaves the burden of
remembrance into a different form,
lore told to the twin girls—
Mary and Martha—

looking into his eyes
as unto a prophecy; his voice
quaking as he speaks—
one song for every little light
going out in his heart.

Desert Fathers

Forcados to Timbuktu
through Korioume or Kabara
will take a day or more.

By our map,
the sandy paths that stretch
from the port to Gao, Djenne,
and Dia also lead to memory.

We respond to what—
between inquest and longing—
called out to us at the beginning,

and join a caravan journeying
into what remains of the city,
what has not become dust.

What witnesses to us first
is not a riff—a kora
or dunun player's lore
told in rhythms.

There are lamentations
swirling in this air;
a gray city's gospel of its blight.

Given the spur of our guide,
what lies ahead,
and the force of this November
afternoon's rhetoric of light,

we hasten to Sankore Madrasah,
past a company of fathers
and their sons—

young scholars, keen as dew,
waving their manuscripts,
lilting their aspirations
and the coming redemption
of this city.

The urgency in their voices,
as of prophecies, interrogating
the hesitations of their fathers,
eyes heavy as stones,

who are pointing back
to those paths where sons,
these boys' age, sold for gold,

once took
and never returned.

A Short Essay on Drowning

in which a freed slave revisits the Zong massacre

With eyes that have known
abysses, ruin, and the soft,
untold ways of water,

he would search the sky
and its mileage of lights for a star or two,
distinct in form—muezzins as they were—
to call us to the essence of each night.

He would start in that space of time
with a glide, yielding us to the
many scenes of rust;

each sigh, a resurrection
of unspeakable things.

And he surely does it well,
leading us, in that pitch of memory,
into the deep of each moment.

Now, he is speaking of Zong,
the memories, its handlers as well,

that voyage across the Atlantic,
from Accra to Black River,
Jamaica, circa 1781.

In our mania
and the fluid of his lore,
something, strong as mojo,
speaks to us, catechising our humanity;
a percussion of love.

Perched on the ensuing hush
is something beyond us,
something outpacing the pulse
of this night and its music of cicada.

So we are thinking of lives,
in aggregates, beyond digits:

The 208 slaves
that made it to Black River.

Those 54 women and children
begging to be spared, screaming
into that November dark.

The drowned men, too—
79 in all,
names hidden
in the directories of the sea.

Here is remembrance beyond the reach of memory.

—TADE IPADEOLA

Noah

Genesis 7:1–15

I sometimes imagine
the hippocampus[1] as an ark,

with varied events walking in,
side by side, like the creatures

you chose in twos
to preserve the animal kingdom.

Here Is Water

At the waterside in Boyo, the
rituals of movement intensify at dusk.

The pull of tides reinvents the shore
into a space for things intimate and lost.

You could find trinket boxes or a girl's
plastic doll in that rubble. Baby shoes, too.

The tiny things are heavier—even songbirds.
I am thinking these tunes being telegraphed

into the dark, fretting the waters,
are a tribute to the lives of drowned men.

I sit by the water, knowing how
sounds could alter the shape of an expanse.

The boys who walk the boundaries now,
in search of collectibles, bear on their bodies

a history threaded to this river.
One wades inward: water around his body;

water, a different texture, in his eyes.
He pulls two of his friends along,

past the quay where the barges
and their fathers' canoes used to lie.

Here is water, he says.
Here is memory shifting in its form,

bearing things heavy and lost. My father
and yours, here now and gone like the tides.

20, Gbogi Street

On my ninth year away from my place of birth

Nostalgic bits of my early years are
of my yellow Jehovah Witnesses'
book of Bible stories,
weekend visits to Bello's *suya* stand

at Metro-Motel,
the Mario video-game challenge,
and our hospice-like compound
that smelt of cow dung fortnightly.

There is a quadruplex to its right.
If you stray into the Casanovas' terrace,
do not pick the rubbery objects
clasping the colored tiles—
they are not balloons.

I remember Decembers, too,
and the firecrackers that heralded Christmas;
the street traders recording every bang
in their purses.

It has been years since we changed address,
so long they gathered in my passé trunk—
my favorite trouser jumped an inch.

Rain Choral

Imvepi refugee settlement, Uganda

Again, a child is the missing letter
in this algebra of grief,

slips out of the company of broken men
furling into a country of themselves.

I watch him meld into the loop of kids
gathered around a relief truck

in a procession of songs.
They join arms, hopping.

It is how they teach a quiet return to love,
these kids shedding weights

their bodies became too frail to bear.
Their litanies echo in the dark,

beseeching days ahead to be kinder.

Numbers

Baga, Northeast Nigeria

Last night, kids here couldn't
gather; so, they muttered elegies
for their game of numbers.
There are more bodies than pebbles.

The Morning After

at an internally displaced people camp in Borno, Northern Nigeria

Only water could bond them
stronger than the kinship of loss,

these little ones
in Rann, far north of Borno,
singing and jumping in the rain—

a respite from the dust
and their parched hearts.

Their ears quick
to thunderclaps weaker
than the booms that claimed
their kindred five months earlier.

Despite that downpour,
the sing-song of school tunes,

the ones they learnt from
UNICEF workers, fill the
spaces hidden from the rain,
from fire.

The morning after,
a girl sits, half awake,

drifted twigs and leaves
around her like mourners,
under the dongoyaro tree
where they had fraternized,

singing the unbroken beatitudes
of rain, lending their voices
to the rhythm of water;

the light in her eyes
weak like the effort of dawn,

her tiny fingers mapping her arms,
the henna drawings darker now,

feeling for an opening,
for the touches of those
she lost to the fire.

Gunfire

Aleppo, Syria

A witness of ash
is what you offer when I ask
if this is your home.

You point to frames
and windowsills widened
by grief.

It was dusk
when we docked at the quay;
darker when you made
for the waters,
fleeing gunfire.

We walk now past the house
and what called out to you—
a fold of postwar kids darting,
chasing moths on the balustrades.

Shuffling your feet through the dust,
twigs, and withering leaves from your past,

you fetch tinders for a different fire.

War Notes

It is in your loss that you learn
the meaning of silence.

The survivors of this war
are all over: the remains of your father,
pre-independence newspapers,
and warfront pictures eulogizing Burma.

Everyone who passes is your relative,
and renewed conversations
are of birdsongs interrupting
monologues around ancestral graves.

Shortly, a lone star will lead you home.

Epitaphs

The last epitaph in Baga was painted
on an empty bottle labeled,
"One for the road."
Booms birth changing sceneries.
Soon, there are mass graves everywhere
with shrubs as landmarks.
Survivors leave, with drunks saying,
"Epitaphs are cheap memories for the dead."

Nightfall, Aleppo

You sit on this porch again;
your legs, swaying,
bestride the banister
where you watch birds swirl—

a tribute to returning refugees,
the Aleppo they knew,
tamarisks, & half-blown buildings

where, before the war,
the birds would perch
for a moment of rest.

They pivot & flap their wings—
a reinvention, a flutter of songs.

It is then you turn from their craft,
the searing rhythm of their oeuvre,
this chorale of the winds.

The ache of nights
coursing through,

you turn instead to moments
you left untended like a field;
the days you lost
or kept for an afterlife.

You remember that evening,
yet again, the dark witness:

how they dragged your mother
into the night, like they
took your rebel father;

her voice, keen, rising
and failing like something
tethered to the wind.

Kites

Rohingya refugee camp in Bangladesh

The camp in Hakimpara
is a moving reel of colors,
skeined images of easterly light.
Beige walls of earth and bamboo
portion the sloped expanse into shelters.
Somewhere in those inventions,
a widow repaints her henna,
lends her songs to dusk.
The remnant of the years she hid
in a vase are blooming into petals.
There is a rare ensemble of kids here—
boys, muezzins calling the world
to their beatitude and the redemption
hidden in paper kites.
The winds lifting their grief,
burdens heavy like love unspoken.

Promenade

I take an evening walk toward this park
with plains like the memories of Sodom.

I do not lose my identity:
I am neither Lot nor the women;

so, I can afford to look back several times.
There are no pillars of salt,

only juvenile lovers radioing
their passions on short wavelength.

The epigraph for "Nightshift at the Coast" is from John Burnside's "After Life."

"All the Little Lights Going Out" is after Warsan Shire.

"All the Little Lights Going Out" and "Pa Cudjo Lewis Weaves a Song" borrow and alter a phrase from the song "All the Little Lights" by Passenger.

"Child of the World" is after Kechi Nomu and Ibukun Adeeko. The epigraph is from Kechi Nomu's poem "Old Bones Are Seeking Wooden Crosses."

"Exodus" is a response to the experience of displaced people leaving Port au Prince, Haiti, by sea after the earthquake in 2010. It borrows and alters from "Circles," a song by Passenger.

"Chorography" is for the people forcefully evicted from Otodo Gbame, Lagos State, Nigeria.

"Pa Cudjo Lewis Weaves a Song" is after Peter Akinlabi.

LEAVING AGADEZ
1. *Emshi* means "leave" in Arabic.

ECLIPSE
1. Bariba, Fon, and Fula are dialects in the Benin Republic.

NOAH
1. Hippocampus is a part of the brain associated with memory.

Fuchsia
Mahtem Shiferraw

Your Body Is War
Mahtem Shiferraw

In a Language That You Know
Len Verwey

Logotherapy
Mukoma Wa Ngugi

When the Wanderers Come Home
Patricia Jabbeh Wesley

*Seven New Generation African
Poets: A Chapbook Box Set*
Edited by Kwame Dawes
and Chris Abani
(Slapering Hol)

*Eight New-Generation African
Poets: A Chapbook Box Set*
Edited by Kwame Dawes
and Chris Abani
(Akashic Books)

*New-Generation African Poets:
A Chapbook Box Set (Tatu)*
Edited by Kwame Dawes
and Chris Abani
(Akashic Books)

*New-Generation African Poets:
A Chapbook Box Set (Nne)*
Edited by Kwame Dawes
and Chris Abani
(Akashic Books)

*New-Generation African Poets:
A Chapbook Box Set (Tano)*
Edited by Kwame Dawes
and Chris Abani
(Akashic Books)

To order or obtain more information on these or other University of
Nebraska Press titles, visit nebraskapress.unl.edu. For more information
about the African Poetry Book Series, visit africanpoetrybf.unl.edu.